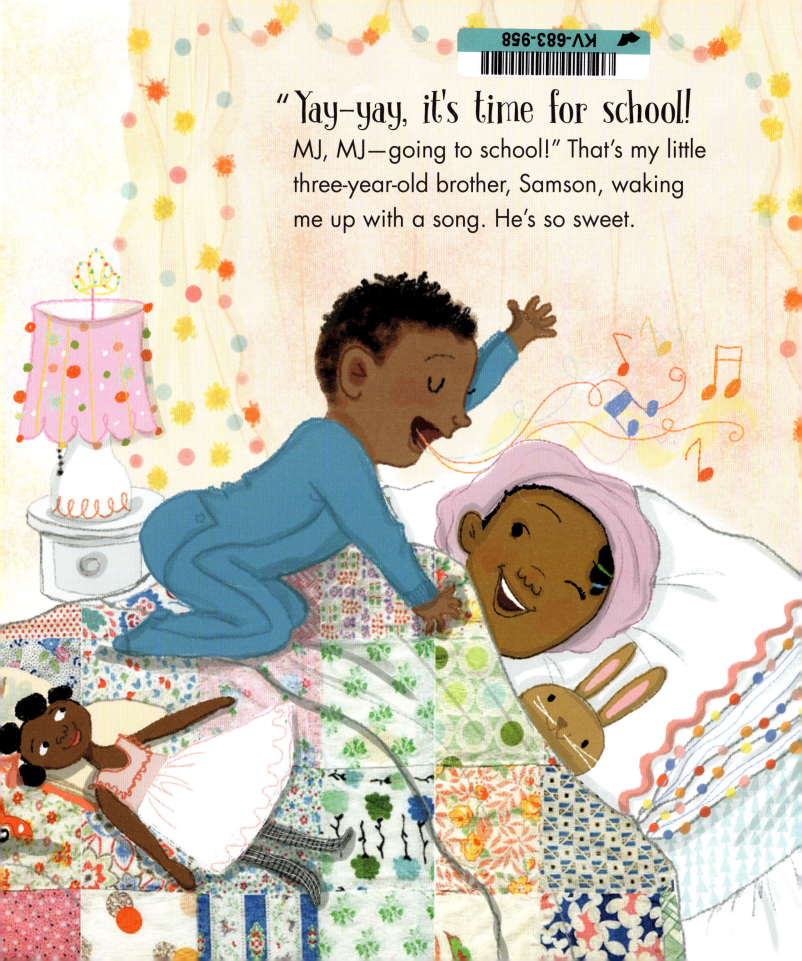

"Yay–yay, it's time for school!
MJ, MJ—going to school!" That's my little
three-year-old brother, Samson, waking
me up with a song. He's so sweet.

Queen of the Classroom

DERRICK BARNES

illustrated by
VANESSA BRANTLEY-NEWTON

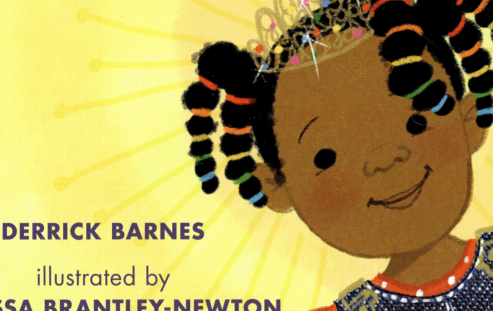

Scallywag Press Ltd

LOND

Children must have at least one person who believes in them. It could be a counselor, a teacher, a preacher, a friend. It could be you. You never know when a little love, a little support, will plant a small seed of hope.

—Marian Wright Edelman

To the memory of Bernette Ford—a true Queen and a pioneer for people of color in publishing. —D.B.

In honor and memory of Floyd Cooper, my mentor and friend. —V.B.-N.

First published in Great Britain in 2022 by Scallywag Press Ltd,
10 Sutherland Row, London SW1V 4JT

Published by arrangement with Nancy Paulsen Books, an imprint of Penguin Young Readers Group,
a division of Penguin Random House LLC

Printed in Glasgow by Bell and Bain

FSC
www.fsc.org
MIX
Paper from responsible sources
FSC® C007785

001

British Library Cataloguing in Publication Data available

978-1-912650-94-1

After bathing, I put on my first day of school outfit. And when I'm dressed, I stand there looking at myself in the mirror, just because I can.

Mama washed and braided my hair last night, and it looks so good!

But she always helps me look nice. Yes, she does.

"MJ, girrrrrrl, did you just step off the cover of a magazine?" Mama says. Then she tells me I'm only missing one thing, and she places a sparkly tiara on my head.

"I wore this on my first day of school," she says. "But today—you will become Queen of the Classroom."

"What does a Queen of the Classroom do, Mama?" I ask.

"First, Queens brighten up every room they enter. Second, Queens are caring and kind.

And third, the good ones are always helpful to others," she says.

I have a good memory, and I am going to remember all of this, for sure!

One. Two. Three!

Then Daddy says, in his deepest voice,
"The royal chariot awaits, Your Highness."
    That means he's ready to take me
to school in his pickup truck.
    I kiss Mama on each cheek,
and we bow to each other.
You know – Queen stuff.

At school, I let Daddy hold my hand and walk me up to the door.

Poor Daddy . . . he doesn't want to leave.

He gives me a big hug, one last look, and then he's gone.

"Welcome, everyone," says our teacher, Miss Lovingood. "Please look for your name card on the desks. That'll be your new home."

I look left—I look right—and there it is . . . **MJ Malone**.

I decorate my name card with drawings of my four favourite things: dolphins, comets, skyscrapers, and my piggy bank.

I get excited when Miss Lovingood says, "Everyone will have their very own task for the entire week."

I know right away which one I want—window monitor.

It'll be my job to open up the blinds and let the sunlight into the room every morning.

Doesn't that sound good?

Plus, brightening up a room is the very first thing that Mama said Queens do, so I'm on it!

But Rayna, the girl sitting next to me,
has her head hung low, looking sad.
"I want to go home . . ."

Right away, I remember Mama saying that Queens
are caring and kind.
  So I reach for Rayna's hands.
  She grabs mine, squeezes, and then gives me a smile.
  And you know what? That makes me feel good, too.

Miss Lovingood calls on me to pick out
a book for the classroom read—
and I find one about a boy getting
a royal haircut.

Later, I help Leo put away the blocks.
Helping is another queenly thing.
One. Two. Three!

For lunch, I have leftover spaghetti—and
guess what? Rayna does too.
   *My mama says there is nothing
wrong with leftovers.* Yum!

I promise to bring Leo some next time, because I love sharing.

At recess, Miss Lovingood teaches us a skipping game called Double Dutch.

Me and a girl named Regina twirl the ropes like twin tornadoes, but it doesn't matter – Miss Lovingood has lightning in her shoes.

We've never seen a grown-up's feet move so fast.

When we go back inside,
we head to the art room.

I make the cutest
picture of Samson.

Then we go to the music room, and I
hit a few high notes for everybody!

And I love sport time, too.
Did I tell you how good I am at football?
Don't let the tiara fool you.

Before it's time to go home, we all sit on the classroom rug that looks like the planet Earth.

We munch, crunch, and nibble on delicious apple slices and sandwich biscuits with strawberry filling.

Miss Lovingood plays soft jazz music like Mama does sometimes. She calls it "wind-down time", and it's a perfect way to end the day.

Back home, I brighten up Samson's day when I give him the picture I made for him, and he plants a sloppy kiss on my cheek.

That boy.

At bedtime, I tell Mama, "I did all the nice queen things you listed."

"You did?! That means you get to keep that tiara. Wear it proudly, MJ."

I will, Mama.
I really will!
MJ . . . Queen of the Classroom . . . that's me.